bounce

wordz & rhythmz

by

stephanie gordon

authorHOUSE™

1663 LIBERTY DRIVE, SUITE 200
BLOOMINGTON, INDIANA 47403
(800) 839-8640
WWW.AUTHORHOUSE.COM

First published by AuthorHouse 12/30/04

ISBN: 1-4208-1748-5 (sc)

Printed in the United States of America
Bloomington, Indiana

This book is printed on acid-free paper.

Thanx to God...the Giver and the Light

For Jazzmin

Table of Contents

entry [undated]

Let my epitaph read that I left a legacy of truth for my own seeds as well as planting a seed of [at least] indifference to cause somebody somewhere to think act or feel real love for another somebody. I wanna bounce from all this 'stuff' of the world and shake loose all the 'heavy'…. be free and be who and what God intends for me to be … how 'bout you?

Election 2004…

I voted today. It was one of the most true and correct things I could do as a new parent, hoping to set an example for my baby girl. I felt blessed to have a choice, blessed but conflicted… I was and still am curious and politically clueless on some of the issues being debated. Puffy is tootin' the "Vote or Die" initiative encouraging young folk to get out and vote….my hope for this new wave of voters is that it's not just a trend or just a fad…consciousness is not fashionable, its inherent and necessary…information and education on and about the issues is imperative {note to self: be more informed}. What *are* our choices? *Who* are the candidates and *what* do they represent. Each year my allergies worsen and my new baby keeps sneezing and wheezing… living in a community with so many refineries blowing smoke, waste and whatever toxins are 'environmentally safe'…what's refined about that? I wanna know why my baby [and so many others] came into this world and immediately developed eczema… momma is courtin' asthma and 1 in 4 of my family is stricken with cancer…can a candidate address that? It must be something in the water or in the air, my neighborhood is sick, my neighbors are fried… I mean, seriously… fireflies went out in '79. What happened to them? So, this rhetoric/wordz and rhythmz is for my baby Jazzmin and the future she will make and be a part of. What evolution of hip hop will she help to usher in…cuz hip hop ain't stoppin'…it's evolving, something like jazz… This year my parents celebrated their 40th wedding anniversary. This year, at 33 years old, I had my first child. This year, I have not smoked one joint. This year, I baked and sold tea cakes to finance this project, finally finishing something I started…everything is about choice… "Bounce" be my voice…listen up…

Reverb

stephanie gordon

Song of the Griot

I have forgotten fireflies
I've forgotten to include
My elders in my prayers
Instead, I relish in the well wishes
Heeded in their prayers for me
I have taken for granted our truths
And our roots
Where and who we come from
…forgotten the songs of our elders
and the songs of our seeds yet to come

these issues would be best addressed
in a Sunday morning solo,
…if only I could sing

Lil red ridin' hood

And somebody said
Everyone isn't deserving,
Goodness at least supposedly,
Is inherent in us all
But somebody said
Not all are deserving

And so, u can call me lil red ridin' hood
And more often than not,
I get lost in the woods
Caught u with the wolf in sheep's clothing
Offering myself up and over
Not believing that all aren't deserving

Traveling this path is hard and lonesome
But still,
There are those of us who believe
True goodness is inherent in us all

The good bye gurl

There she goes again
Running a bath
Lighting the candles
Smoking a square
Alone in her queendom
mean from fighting those demons
That only comes at night
When she's alone
This gurl be like
Good bye.
While she be trippin'
Still sittin' wit chickens
{they don't fly}
there she goes again
creating ritualistic habitual trix
her perfect superficial fix
gettin' gone/catchin' hell
especially when she alone
the gurl be like
good bye.

EWF (earth wind & fire) reprise

Open our eyes
Love all mankind
No color, no breed
No allegiance, no creed
Division keeps us blind
We're all tryin' to climb
From the depths of our minds
Conditioned into beliefs & traditions
Which needs rearranging
...times are changing
but remaining stagnant...divided
we've missed the point of Love
...heaven (?) ...ain't it here
on earth?

Zoom. I'm stretching the corners of my mind to find some semblance of freedom. I'm looking back only to move forward, learning from the choices I've made and the experiences I've had lends me strength to improve, leaving room only for growth... only to Zoom.

The foreigner

Lately, I've been thinkin' of
Packin' it in
Closin' up shop
Retreating to my in/land
An island of thoughts anyway

Decisive by nature?
Ha!
Any other attempts at explanations
Of the actions of this world soul
Would be futile, even in a poem

Everyday gets closer 2 home
Like how my hips keep on spreadin'
Knowing their predestined position
On the timeline, anyway
When I'm forever tryin' 2 keep up with mine
Get real close 2 earth,
Know it/be it
Synchronize my clock
With its definitive tick tock; rotation

Feeling and knowing deeper
The meaning of a thing
A precious fool, I stand b4 U
Asking 2 be pardoned for my constant slips
Into obscurity
Supposedly/superficially removed
From the ways of this world

Baby momma drama

The women must be crazy….and so are most of the men.
I've gained the title
"Baby momma"
And he gets a cookie,
Crowned "baby daddy"
Give him a cookie
For being and doin' what he's supposed to
Bein' there…givin' a damn

That ain't typical
That ain't expected

Hold onto that man
Guurrrrl, u bettah be glad he's willin'…
No matter how…
No matter what…
Cuz the physical ain't the only tangible
I ought to be thankful
Stand up and give applause
For the brotha who didn't pause
To stand up for his own…
The sistas must be crazy
For some of the advice that they gave me
Hold onto that man
No matter how much he…
Now matter what he…
No matter ….no matter…no matter what
Hold onto that MAN…*it ain't typical*…
I'd laugh if it wasn't so pitiful
So…give the brotha a cookie
For doin' what he's supposed to

Supaflygurl: the interview

Might u be a part of my clan
A lost member of my tribe…my kind
In this lifetime, it's my turn
To be on top, to be Air
{I know u don't care}
Uncertain of which way I'll blow next
This time, might u have enuff earth
To make mud pies with me

How 'bout wearing the 's' on your chest
For a change, and…would u save *me*
Could u be good for sumthin
other than nuttin'
Could u count me as one
Maybe even first
What if I stopped flyin' at night
Creamin' in your dreams
Could u love me again
Like in a dream/but make it real this time

Might u be a part my clan
A lost member of my tribe
If so, good seein' u again

Drama queen (be)

Maybe I like it
I must like it
This constant tilt-a-whirl
Somehow, the title
Keeps me clearly defined
Otherwise
What would my existence be
Or mean

Who would I be
If peace came
Tasting like peaches and cream

"drama queen"

lady of the labyrinth

In the near/distant reality
Flowing freely
She creates her own…
Crazy all day/every day
Howling @ the moon
Walking the labyrinth
Her mission, to remover her Jahfusion
Accelerating our ascension
But it jut comes out low and mixed
And that be the opposite of ascent

There the love message exists
Within prophetic hope quilts
Lyrical graffiti poems of paradise lost
Space and time don't mean a thing

sky

my sky is blue
so what do u think
should I cry u some cream
and think it to pink

should I save the rose
from red to rust
should I choose the garden
for them and for us

my sky is falling
so you'd think I could catch
catch it by the heels
above the strawberry patch
don't rustle me no rose
from red to rust
don't sugar coat my truth
for them and for us

if my sky must fall
then let it be known
I kept my truth
Until it was full grown

stephanie gordon

Rebound

at some point...
I decided to drink my soul sober
And take from the fountain of forever...
Becuz it's mine for the taking

mercy

humanity overrules Christianity
and I'm sure God is laughing
at what was already known
[u big dummy]
that which took us so long
to realize…
typically allowing the other puppeteer
to warden over our existence
a fiery one no doubt…
living sleepwalking thru a life sentence
of misery
let go…zoom… bounce

mercy
found myself trippin' on truth
excused myself allowing the Love
and the Light to live and shine'

ghosts of the familiar

I'm reminded or rather wounded
By thoughts of the memories
Of the warmth of his body lying next to me
Ghosts of the familiar creeps up 2 me
Temptin' me/testin' me
Tellin' me I'm stronger than I used 2 be
Convincing me that it be all about me

Father may I
Bask in your glory a little longer
Until I get a little stronger

Ghosts of the familiar blows smoke up my toke
And I choke on the Truth that binds me
Flesh tryin' its best to overrule me
This despondent dreamer
Prays for grace and patience

Father may I
Be sustained by your infinite High, everlasting
By and by

I dare not fall asleep...once more
Unconsciously becoming a wallflower pilgrim
Haunted by ghosts of the familiar

letting go...

Co-dependency issues have held me back from achieving and prospering in my own life. It's an issue that I still struggle with daily. One of the co-dependent relationships I've tagged was [is] with marijuana. I had to learn not to become overwhelmed and controlled by the high. I needed not to be so dependent on the smoke, which blinded me to truth...*which certainly does set u free...*

My love affair with ganja, herb, sensimellia, smoke, weed or whatever lovely nickname we give it, was and still is a weakness, which I battle almost daily. The lovely high it offered to me gave me peace of mind and a relaxation that was unequaled to any other experience or feeling I'd ever known. Marijuana allowed me to think and write and compose poetic poetry and prose, unveiling deep and philosophical thoughts and opinions on this-that and the other. But what I came to realize, was that marijuana for me, was an escape or a crutch to ignore or not deal with real life issues, which presented themselves to me. I refused to deal with even the simplest life issues... forget tackling the bigger ones. The answer to all the peace I sought was rolled up in a blunt or a fat joint. All I needed was some fire and I'd blaze away whatever ailed me, or welcomed the temporary bliss the sess offered to me. This was my refuge. This was my peace. Nothing and no one else mattered to me, least of all, myself.

Montego Bay, Jamaica '02

If we can be physically close to God, then this was a time when
I truly felt near and close to Him. Montego Bay, Jamaica. Sheryl
Lee Ralph's second annual Jamerican Film Festival. This was truly
a blessed trip. An up and coming Jamaican musician introduced
himself to me as Abijah and blessed me with his *revelation*/ his
testimony of his Walk as a Christian. We spoke on love, life
and poetic muses. Poet to poet we talked. What was I missing
as a writer that blocked me from flowing like I knew I could? I
posed the question to the peaceful and talented musician and
he responded, speaking so eloquently with conviction about a
Love far greater than carnal love could ever relate and far higher
than weed could ever smoke me away. I wanted to reach my
full potential...I knew I had to let up on the smoke, but more
importantly, I wanted to know Him.

Rock-Steady . I've realized I have to grab hold to the shaky foundation on which I stand [evolution is ongoing] my ass backward plans to stand on my own will forever be the scarlet letter of a madwoman. **Zoom. Let go and bounce.** My freedom rests at my fingertips, and my faith says to let go and let loose with it. The antidote to shake off this "sleep" which holds me idle lies in the belief that His word is borne…His word is bond… believe in myself and move…. zoom and *bounce*…

Free Shine

If I was comprised of magic and mars
I'd feed u these eyes
I'd feed u these stars
So u can see
The Light that shines
Ain't just for me
This love be free
Be deep like mobb
Be great like God
Be shine
...it ain't just mine

cycles

It started at 15
These cycles and patterns
Of self-destructive misrepresentations
Of love...lost

It started at 15
Whose life/ what life
Was really terminated
Wasn't that the beginning
And this is the end.... to the beginning?

It started at 15
Felt more like thunder without the rain
Although I wished it would...rain
Come down and wash away the scars
Come down and wash away the shame
It started at 15
I've decided to finish what I started
Breaking these cycle and patterns
Of lost love

A funky love poem

This is a funky love poem
Written at about 4 a.m.
Born on a cold/hard bathroom floor

This is a funky love poem
Written at about 4 a.m.
Born from the soul of my 'eye'
And I am cryin' 'why?'

This is a poem about sistahood
Becuz I am afraid of being alone at night
And lately I haven't slept a wink
Thinkin' about my sistas
And something t.d. jakes said
About the daughters of Israel
U/me
Missing/bleeding
Fussin' about our female condition
Hollerin' about how the grass is always greener
For the brothas/for anotha sista
Thinkin' she's got it better
Thinkin' she's got it together

This is a cold-hearted stanky ass love poem
Written at about 4 a.m.
Born on a cold/hard bathroom floor
Mixing pink pill with blue pill
Separating Up pill from Down pill
Celebrating this new pill
That just might get me well

This is a poem about sistahood
Becuz I do not want my epitaph to read,

stephanie gordon

'she did not care to share'
that I am afraid of being alone at night
bearing witness on a cold/hard bathroom floor
a dizzied up head, a mixed up soul
praying for some peace of mind
some kindred kindness
from anotha sista, who just might call
to say that she cares to share..
a funky love poem
about sistahood
at about 4 a.m.

recycle

This house is alive again
With healing and passion
Progression, once a stagnant hope
An easy dream, fixed on night terrors

This house is alive again
With laughter and spirit
The walls breathe and sigh relief
Then braces for the next storm

This house is alive again
The knowing each other
The loving each other
Growing together
This is a family
Alive, again

The Christian contradiction

INI/ by and by
My benevolence be my soul/be my whole contradiction
My goodness been searchin' for food 2 be fed
Even diggin' those dark places instead…
My goodness been lackin'/slackin'
Jackin' 4 shallow beats
Searching those highs that kept me low
Idle confusion coddles my curious soul
Slows my pen/slows my Walk 2 a stammer
Stagnating 2 long in humanity's woes
My search for Water leads to groove theories
Weary for Truth

I may have slipped
But I didn't fall
I may have slipped
But I'm mindin' my call
Grace found me wandering
Down by the fence of indifference
Once upon a time & again
When I've lost my way
My pen leads as well as my womb bleeds
The philosophies of a female/Christian/poet
Stray ones like me need contradictions like these
Ain't gonna let Jah*fusion come between I and Thee
INI/by and by
Benevolence be my whole
Be my soul…contradiction

Induction [journal entry]

Feels like thunder more than rain...I have a knot in my throat that won't go away. It hurts to swallow. The baby will be here at least by Wednesday. My doctor will be inducing labor beginning tomorrow (Monday). I'm 36 weeks. Although I'm anxious to meet my little darling, I'm so scared.... My life is about to change so drastically in just a few hours. The anticipation is so surreal... I must be crazy, single motherhood {WOW}... I didn't plan it this way... I won't believe it until she's here. I pray that she's okay.

Divine

Earthbound
Landlocked and thirsty
My search for groove Water
Translates into groove theories
Weary for truth
And your devil must be weary
From worryin' over mine
U hit me on the left one
And I just turn to my irie side
Certainly, he is busy
Using idle fools
Stud'n the other man's blues
With no thought of lending a hand
Or offering a prayer
For self or for mankind

His love is Divine

4 all them things and everything
I put up and ovah
Knowing all those things
Are possible thru Christ
Who strengthens me

stephanie gordon

Tea cake

I'm laughing at how domestic I've become
Baking tea cakes
Measuring flour and sugar
Exacting measurements
Exchanging recipes and old wives tales
About colic and chamomile remedies
And I swear my own identity
Has gotten mixed up in between butter
And sugar and nutmeg
My breast have become teats
And I seemed to have misplaced my vagina
Cuz it ain't workin' not even for solitaire
I'm laughing at myself...
Baking and selling tea cakes
...and enjoying it

Ride

My 'g' light is on;
So does that mean go?

Head on collision
Forever itchin' my 'g' spot
Alone

The water be too cold
To just jump in
Don't it?

Forward march. Girl.
Up and over
To the other side of the Mount;
I'm bound for/to Glory

I should know,
My 'g' light is on
And that means go

curse wordz

u cursed us
with your unkind wordz
of old school thought
swordz used to abuse
but never once taught
love

never gonna be nuthin
never gonna make sumthin...
...niggas
always be like crabz in a bucket

some of us still bleed from your wordz
some of us believed in your curses
swordz like those cut to the bone
swordz like those cut to the bone
and live on and on
roll on and on in cycles

but ain't that what u prophesied?
ain't that what u meant/your cruel intent?
mean things aimed at your own seeds
those princes meant to be kings
baby girls meant to be queens
grown into those sorry ass sumthins
no good for nuthins
u bore in to breed more misery
it sho nuff luvs company

the miseducation of eve

her nature is cravin
x chromosome misbehaving
jumpin thru hoops
zig-zaggin and missin the root
of her true confusion
a seed we [all] instilled and inspired
miseducating eve

beautiful, in all ways but spiritual

her ways and actions
aggressively and maybe even passively
show and prove her training,
conditioned to believe in
the punanny propaganda provided
by those examples b4 her
teaching her use
the deepness betwixt her thighs
cuz it be her best prize
and all she has to offer

beautiful, in all ways but spiritual

stephanie gordon

Recognize

stephanie gordon

Could I write a line to set myself free
Could I write a real rhyme without smoking a tree
Knowledge be borne
Knowledge be high
Wisdom be the apple/be the storm of my eye

straight shoota

keep shootin' til u get it straight
til u get it right
so high…high…high
u fly right into yo'self
back into love
…and I give up,
not on you, but on me…

holdin' on much too long
to that monkey on our backs
the one that's got u all cracked up
the one that got me all jacked up
and stale
I'm tired, aren't u?
Binging again…
Existing in a paradox
Of go, stop, rock steady
Yes, no…eyes wide shut
In a not quite existence
Shootin' half cocked
…not

I gotta move
But I'm here…always
If u ever wanna know
Who's lovin' u…it's us and Him
Love ya, keep straight shootin'
Til u fly back home

I'm lettin' go
This one be… bounce(able)

This is just another battle....the war's already been waged
[won]....and it ain't mine to meddle with...just maintain...
pray away the pain...Higher Power is what I claim
Living life lovely....pushin' to reach the next level

Jive talkin'

Is sisterhood really powerful?
I doubt it;
The cattiness of/between women
Distresses me

I've become accustom to the idea
Of being alone and being on guard
Within sisterhood
…am I paranoid?

I've been known to question
The loyalty of women
While claimin' feministic stylistics
Holdin' high a righteous fist
The other tightly grippin'
My beautiful bronzed 5 speed
(batteries included)

Yeah, I've envied
The loyalty expressed in relationships
Between menfolk
Customized handshakes, secret codes
Dap dap dap
Supposedly anyway

But now, I've grown accustomed to
Treadin' life alone
Without sistafriends
Sharing poetry and coffee
Jive talkin' with God/with me
We are kool like that
Always…
Dap dap dap

gurl talk

there is no honor among thieves
on reflection of relationships
among women, catty [at best]
speakin' from my own self[ish] past
I have taken her heartsong
took it and invalidated it
Scoffed and pointed @ it
Left her exposed and vulnerable
Selfishly…
I shared her secrets
Showing her thin skin to whomever
Might want to pick it apart
That's what I did….
Selfishly becoming a part of the problem
Givin' up my friend girl…my gurlfriend
For cheap seats…eating and throwin popcorn
From the mezzanine….ain't that a nigga heaven?
I apologize…

bright pink lips
[stargazer gloss #5]

bright pink lips
love demonology
so-called intellectual philosophies
that fly above the heads
of ditzy chicks
perceived to be a cinch
to ease into easiness

simple

bright pink lips
love misconceptions about sexiness
and fools who address
bright pink lips with only
thoughts of wetness
bright pink lips love being taken
for granted, kissed anyway
while speaking feministic specials
blue lighted while constructing poems
exactly opposite from
dignified signifyin' monkeys
with their pointless pencils
preaching popcorn, bubble gum psalms
flexing linguistic muscles
which these bright pink lips
could speak better literately
easily
consciously
with love,
from bright pink lips

supaflybrotha

And so Jesus wept…

So brotha…why can't u?
weakness doesn't exist
In the exhibition of emotion
By a man

Compassion. Affection.
The definition of strength
Is within your tears

…and so Jesus wept
and he was a Supabrotha
so brotha, why can't u?

alert

my tv is totally pc
electric with televised revolutions
orange
yellow
red...white ...blue
on high alert

homeland security threatened
Middle man meddlin'
Us/them/Hatians
Living the American scream
In a global nightmare on *your* street

The candidates debate
[are these my choices?]
war...intelligence
who makes the most sense?

Alert

Choice...choices...choose

Render

stephanie gordon

Buffalo Gurl [poem 1]

My own freaky behavior touches 2 close to truth
2 close 2 the edge at times
I be a buffalo gurl… on the outside
I being she
Reminiscing on how she used to get free
…in bondage
this Christianity insanity
Is insane…let go of the smoke
Toke on God fire
denomination division creates indecision
within me
their hypocrisy [in] humanity
leaves me scratcin' my head
tryin' to understand
…*lean not onto my own*
standin' on the outside
hopin' to get free…
thru Christianity

Buffalo Gurl [poem 2]

I was ….she is
Missin/fixed/twisted
Spittin' pink champale tales
Aimlessly chunkin' dimes
Into her wishin' well

A ragged abused temple
Confused

This lil light of mine
I shine
Earthquakes I find in my mind
I've died again
Butterflied outta my hazy phase
Elevatin' to my crazy phase
And these days
I'm flyin' so sunglass high
Got me wondering why
I didn't try "G" first
As opposed to the lows
Those days I suppose
Have truth and purpose
found myself trippin' on truth
excused myself allowing the Love
and the Light to live and shine'

all the time...

I heard my own distress call. Shallow but deep, dark but full of light. Faithless, hopeless...loveless. I knew there was a better life for me somewhere out there amidst all that fog and murk. I was just floating along, being pushed and pulled wherever the dark current pushed me...and I really didn't care.

saved?

I'm wondering if I'm still here
Have I floated to the top
{superficial people float to the top}
or have a sank to the bottom
{am I too heavy to coast}
I'm trippin' on truth
What is real
What is correct

Does righteousness exist only in action
Even if that action is fixed?

I'm existing
But not

I'm lost
But I found
…I miss paradise

zig – zag flag

this window offers a romantic view
it swings sweet music and breeze
it offers to me daffodils trumpeting peace
this view transcends so-called reality
getting down to roots
of how and why Truth chin-checked Miss Liberty
4 now, I'm in a native way
recalling nevermind reparations
remembering the Navajo
reciting the Negro National Anthem
as opposed 2 star spangled banners
stately, I prefer sweet potato to apple pie

peace is on the tip of my mind
and I wonder, would it be un-American
to be against it – War – that is
denying the realness of names and numbers
of our own, who should be at home
welcoming Spring

What is my position on the war?
Hussein's pit bull determination?
Bush's egotistical mania?
I'd rather be diggin' on ice cream sandwiches
As surely as our troops
Could/would dig it instead of diggin' and sleepin'
In trenches

???
where is the love?
Is there really an escape that's morally straight?
This/it would be an arrival at what?
4 what? 4 who?

stephanie gordon

We find answers/solutions in purple hazes
Sippin' syrup crazes/extacy raves/wet water/fry rages
The whole home of the brave is
Waving the flag, while rollin' a fatty
Breeze it/smoke it all away
This window offers a romantic view
My only wish, to be higher than this

temptation

I grasped his kind
Not soon enuff
But not 2 late
To roll up my cuffs
And flee

Gurl Hurricane Jane

Again I wait
And watch the clock
But my wait and prayers
Don't seem stronger than that want
Of that rock…
Cocaine is her name
Blowin' thru like hurricane jane
Her game is strong
Her lines definitely be
Stronger than mine
Plottin' her path
Blowin high winds…high tides
[and jadakiss said it's almost over] *why?*

hurricane gurl
blowin' thru my family
my community
leaving us naked and at her mercy
waitin' on that breaking point
what maniac would create this manmade hate
disguised as love
the hopeful, but faithless
the determined, but loveless

faith…be the way
hope…be the light
love…be the antidote
and I hope someday
u know that your seawall
be Great enuff…

all day anyway

untitled

Tryin' to touch my soul again
Pick up the pen
B4 I explode again
…lean on not my own
but kneel and leave it
like burdens be known to be
…down by the river side
I wonder will these float or sink
Ride on a wave and coast til
I truly let it go…

walk

accepting the realities of life
and the living is easy;
I choose peace instead of agony, today
She be steppin' on the toes of angels, instead
She be singin' of the road up ahead
The one less traveled;
Scary, but the living is easy

Spiderman

U think nobody knows who u are

U are an addict
Addicted to the rise and the fall
U climb and descend
Crash, anty up to do it all again
Night after night
Day after day
U think nobody knows who u are
But its u…naked and exposed
Spiderman…
Where are u going to?

One love

this Jah fusion
confusion and division
hinders the high
hypocrisy is spelled with a capital H
scrawled in bold black letters
bigger and deffer than those
that spell Christianity
...still life and love moves along always
God be an infinite stream of consciousness
Definitely...

On denomination...

what does it matter
what kinda wings u got
as long as u take flight
this Jah fusion is neither the way nor the Light

the conscious youth crochets
hip-hop hope quilts for paradise lost
and I'm hopeful
that this Love wave hits the most...
who's been missin' it
cooperate instead of separate
folk who just might need it
right now

stephanie gordon

Reveal

I come from women

I come from women
I come from strong women
Been thru the storm women
Heroin/horse/Demerol y'all
Is a mutha
I come from café women
Loud women
Beer drinkin' women
I come from sad women
Broken-hearted women
I come from cotton field women
Hot water cornbread women
I come from runaway slave women
Mammy/jezebel/brave women
I come from ignorant women confused women
Natural women
Western women
Pretty women
Sexy women
I come from single mother women
Suffering women
I come from my women, my sistas…
I come from u
I come from women
Black power/ungowa women
I come from deep women
Wise women/hard women
And not-so-smart women
Becuz being smart was not a part
Of the women I come from
I come from women
I come from beautiful women
Co-dependent women/ganga addicted women

stephanie gordon

Simple women
Sleeping, slumbering women
I come from awakened women
Spirit filled women
Living water wanting women
I come from wailing women
Tea cake/7 up cake baking women
I come from women who marched
Women who struggled
Women who fought and were bought
Laid and prayed
Women who healed and kneeled
Weeping for u and for me
My sistas, I come from u
And u from me

I come from women

Manifest Destiny

Have we lost u to the world?
My faith wanes
As I whisper once more
'a prayer for the Ephesians'
a holy hope for u and for me

is that crave for that high
pimpin' u so low
so wide and long and so deep
u can't feel love, f'sho

I don't know u
We don't know u
Love knows u
who are u?
your eyes are desolate holes
of pain – a slave
your ways and actions are
crafty and robotic
driven/directed
full with devious worldly indulgence
makes me wanna holla
makes me wanna cry
makes me wanna give up
are my prayers in vain?

I don't know u
U are stranger, even to yourself
But love knows u

Guilty pleasures

I let him in again
To dine fabulously on my flesh
Abandoning fresh soul
For commercialized hip-hop

Easy

The attic

The walls of my father's house
are bleeding/leaking
Bulging at the seams
To shout whispers which
Have housed and hidden stale truths
I'm not supposed to remember
But I do
The truth sho nuff
Come to life/comes to light
To heal all things, in time

supaflygurl [raw]

Nursing scotch on the rox
Cut with lime
...and lies
maligned and manipulated
by my womanhood....buy my womanhood
it is for sale [no matter how it's played]
even prettied up/strengthened up
in a strong black gurl poem
like this one...
pretending to be hard and hip
Proposing to be medium well
when it's typically raw
unclothed...unfinished...undone

she be a...

Sleeping dragon
Fighting demons
Sippin smart martinis
In mid December, if I remember correctly
Sitting directly under thunder and lightning
...a storm in the gulf of my familiar, brewing
But purple oleanders line
My imperfect seawall all day anyway

...all day anyway
all day anyway
all day anyway

Come, black macho

His independence
Slips thru these fingertips
Like the sands of time
meanwhile he's constantly crawlin'
Back up into mine…

My womb is wanting
Waiting, warm and ready
For his seed
To define me again as Wo-man

come, black macho
Show me your strength
So that I can define mine

Cannibalistic

I wanted to marry
Dress my bridegroom up
In my dreams
I was a man eater
Steady building him up
Just to tear him down
Keep him in his place
For me to have and to hold
Push him away
When he got too close
I was lying in wait
Nesting and keeping score
Playing lightly his manhood
Devilishly relishing at his chaos
Pricking at his inability to produce
Or reproduce
Reminding him of his manly responsibilities
Drilling home his shortcomings,
To dim those of my own

I was a man eater
I wanted him shackled to me
And my dreams of happily ever after
My picket fence sense was perfect

Egg drop soup

Covered in madness...
Gladly will I take cover
Easily inheriting
A hollow heirloom deeper than mobb
Lacking truth, lacking God
Passed down from a liner lineage/a legacy
Honestly parallel parking between
Insanity and so-called reality
Addictive behaviors shroud me
Ganja, be a realized spinoff to Zoloft

Covered in madness...
Gladly will I take cover
Sleepwalking, basically being basic all day
Allowing baseheads to be architectures of my dreams
Paralysis...based in fear
Will I forever wallow in this misery?
Covered in madness
Peaked as weakness
Gladly will I take cover...

tea cake recipe

makes 4 dozen

ingredients

2 cups butter softened
2 cups sugar
3 eggs
2 T. buttermilk
5 cups all-purpose flour
I t. baking soda
dash of salt
tiny drop lemon extract
I t. vanilla extract

Cream butter and sugar beating well. Add eggs one at a time beating well after each addition. Add buttermilk and beat well. Combine dry ingredients [flour, soda, salt] gradually stir into creamed mixture. Stir in vanilla and lemon extracts. Knead dough well. Let dough set for several hours [preferably overnight]. Roll to 1/4 inch thickness on floured surface, cut into rounds with cookie cutter. Place I inch apart on lightly greased cookie sheet. Bake at 400F for 8 minutes or until lightly browned.

About the Author

Stephanie Gordon is a beat street poet with grass roots appeal. She is a locally *(Houston)* celebrated poet whose writing style is charged with love for humanity. She describes her writing style as a combination of *'poetic truth, hip hop blues and rock-steady soul.* Her poetry has appeared in several national and local publications. She occasionally shares her work at open mic venues in the Houston area. She baked and sold tea cakes to help finance publishing costs to make "bounce" a reality. Stephanie is a proud Southerner with a heart as big as Texas with raw talent just as bold. She is a personal care provider and homemaker, raising her baby girl in the southern part of Texas.